Una visita a/A Visit to

La estación de bomberos/The Fire Station

por/by B. A. Hoena

Editor Consultor/Consulting Editor: Dra. Gail Saunders-Smith

Consultor/Consultant: Jennifer Norford, Senior Consultant
Mid-continent Research for Education and Learning
Aurora, Colorado

Capstone
press®

Mankato, Minnesota

Pebble Plus is published by Capstone Press
151 Good Counsel Drive, P.O. Box 669, Mankato, Minnesota 56002.
www.capstonepress.com

1 2 3 4 5 6 12 11 10 09 08 07

Library of Congress Cataloging-in-Publication Data
Hoena, B. A.
  [Fire station. Spanish]
  La estación de bomberos/por B.A. Hoena = The fire station/by B.A. Hoena.
  p. cm.—(Una visita a = A visit to)
  Parallel title: Fire station
  Includes index.
  Spanish and English.
  ISBN-13: 978-1-4296-0072-9 (hardcover : alk. paper)
  ISBN-10: 1-4296-0072-1 (hardcover : alk. paper)
  ISBN-13: 978-1-4296-1195-4 (softcover pbk.)
  ISBN-10: 1-4296-1195-2 (softcover pbk.)
  1. Fire stations—Juvenile literature. 2. Fire stations. I. Title. II. Title: Fire station.
TH9148.H6718 2008
628.9'25—dc22   2006100171

Summary: Simple text and photos present a visit to a fire station—in both English and Spanish.

Interactive ISBN-13: 978-0-7368-7912-5
Interactive ISBN-10: 0-7368-7912-9

Editorial Credits
Sarah L. Schuette, editor; Katy Kudela, bilingual editor; translations.com, translation services; Eida del Risco,
    Spanish copy editor; Jennifer Bergstrom, set designer

Photo Credits
Capstone Press/Gary Sundermeyer, all

Pebble Plus thanks the New Ulm Fire Department, New Ulm, Minnesota, for the use of its
department during photo shoots.

Note to Parents and Teachers

The Una visita a/A Visit to set supports national social studies standards related to the
production, distribution, and consumption of goods and services. This book describes
and illustrates a visit to a fire station in both English and Spanish. The images support
early readers in understanding the text. The repetition of words and phrases helps early
readers learn new words. This book also introduces early readers to subject-specific
vocabulary words, which are defined in the Glossary section. Early readers may need
assistance to read some words and to use the Table of Contents, Glossary, Internet Sites,
and Index sections of the book.

Table of Contents

Tabla de contenidos

The Fire Station

A fire station is a fun

place to visit.

La estación de bomberos

Visitar la estación de bomberos

es un paseo divertido.

4

NEW ULM

Trucks and Gear

Fire engines have flashing
lights and loud horns.
Fire engines and other trucks
park in the bay.

Camiones y equipo

El carro de bomberos tiene luces
brillantes y una sirena muy ruidosa.
El carro de bomberos y otros
camiones se estacionan en la bahía.

Some fire trucks carry
ladders. Ladders can reach
the tops of tall buildings.

Algunos carros de bomberos
tienen escaleras. Las escaleras
alcanzan las azoteas de edificios
muy altos.

Firefighters wear coats,
helmets, and boots.
The heavy gear keeps
them safe.

Los bomberos usan chaquetas,
cascos y botas resistentes.
Con este equipo están protegidos.

Around the Fire Station

Dispatchers tell firefighters

how to get to a fire quickly.

Dispatchers listen to radios,

read maps, and answer calls.

En la estación de bomberos

Los operadores les dicen a los bomberos

cómo llegar a los incendios rápidamente.

Los operadores escuchan el radio,

leen mapas y contestan llamadas.

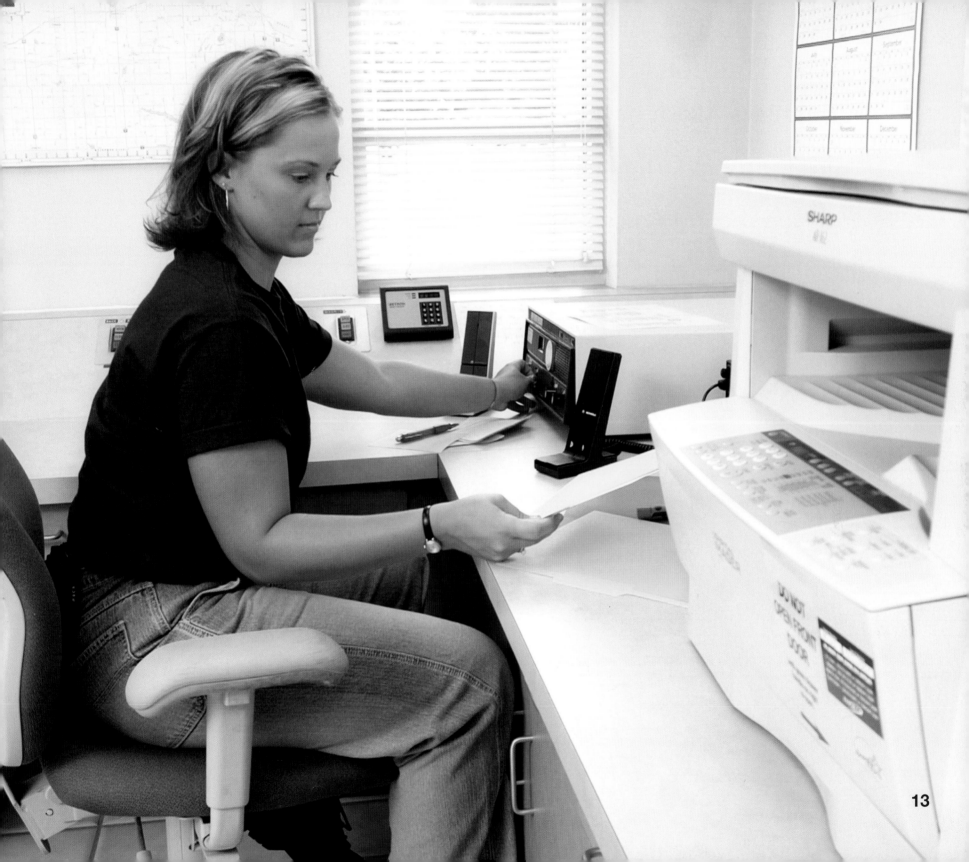

SHARP

13

Firefighters learn in the
training room. They hear
and see how to use new
safety equipment.

Los bomberos aprenden en la sala
de entrenamiento. Allí escuchan
y ven cómo se utiliza el nuevo
equipo de seguridad.

Firefighters exercise in
the dorm during the day.
They rest in beds at night.

Los bomberos se ejercitan
durante el día en su dormitorio.
Por la noche, descansan
en sus camas.

Firefighters cook meals
in the kitchen. They
eat together during breaks.

Los bomberos cocinan su comida
en la cocina. Se sientan juntos
a la hora comer.

Working Together

People at the fire station
work together to keep
their community safe.

Trabajo en equipo

En la estación de bomberos todos
trabajan juntos para mantener
a su comunidad segura.

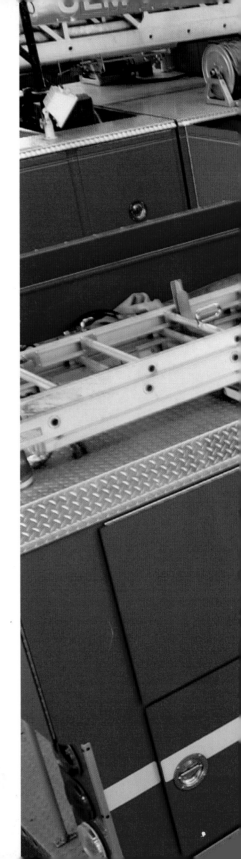

Glossary

bay—the area in a fire station where trucks and other firefighting equipment is kept; the bay is on the ground floor so that trucks can drive onto the street.

dorm—a room or a building with beds; another word for dorm is dormitory.

fire engine—a large truck that carries firefighting equipment to a fire; firefighters also ride on fire engines.

gear—a set of clothing or equipment; firefighters wear heavy coats, pants, and boots called bunker gear.

truck—a vehicle; fire stations use many different kinds of trucks; pumper trucks carry and pump water; ladder trucks carry tall ladders to fires.

Glosario

la bahía—área en la estación de bomberos donde se
guardan los camiones y el equipo contra incendios.
La bahía está en la planta baja de manera que los
camiones puedan salir hacia la calle

el camión—un vehículo grande, las estaciones de
bomberos utilizan distintos tipos de camiones;
los camiones de bombeo llevan agua y la bombean;
los camiones escalera llevan escaleras altas
a los incendios

el carro de bomberos—camión grande que lleva
el equipo contra incendios hacia el incendio, también
lleva a los bomberos

el dormitorio—habitación o edificio con camas

el equipo—la ropa especial de los bomberos: chaquetas,
pantalones y botas muy resistentes

Internet Sites

FactHound offers a safe, fun way to find Internet sites related to this book. All of the sites on FactHound have been researched by our staff.

Here's how:

1. Visit *www.facthound.com*

2. Choose your grade level.

3. Type in this book ID **1429600721** for age-appropriate sites. You may also browse subjects by clicking on letters, or by clicking on pictures and words.

4. Click on the **Fetch It** button.

FactHound will fetch the best sites for you!

Index

Sitios de Internet

FactHound te brinda una manera divertida y segura de encontrar sitios de Internet relacionados con este libro. Hemos investigado todos los sitios de FactHound. Es posible que algunos sitios no estén en español.

Se hace así:

1. Visita *www.facthound.com*

2. Elige tu grado escolar.

3. Introduce este código especial **1429600721** para ver sitios apropiados a tu edad, o usa una palabra relacionada con este libro para hacer una búsqueda general.

4. Haz un clic en el botón **Fetch It**.

¡FactHound buscará los mejores sitios para ti!

Índice